ROCKFORD PUBLIC LIBRARY

3 1112 017730140

W9-BJL-686

WITHDRAWN

J 940.3072 ROS
Ross, Stewart
World War I

Kid Pick!

Title: _____

Author: _____

Picked by: _____

Why I love this book:
_____
_____
_____
_____

Please return th...
Mrs Heather...
your revie...
hgunne...

ROCKFORD PUBLIC LIBRARY

Rockford, Illinois

www.rockfordpubliclibrary.org

815-965-9511

Research It!

World War I

Stewart Ross

Heinemann Library
Chicago, Illinois

ROCKFORD PUBLIC LIBRARY

www.heinemannraintree.com
Visit our website to find out more information about Heinemann-Raintree books.

To order:
☎ Phone 888-454-2279
🖷 Visit www.heinemannraintree.com to browse our catalog and order online.

© 2010 Heinemann Library
an imprint of Capstone Global Library, LLC
Chicago, Illinois

All rights reserved. No part of this publication may be reproduced or transmitted in any form or by any means, electronic or mechanical, including photocopying, recording, taping, or any information storage and retrieval system, without permission in writing from the publisher.

Edited by Andrew Farrow and Helen Cannons
Designed by Steven Mead
Illustrated by Stefan Chabluk,
 ©Capstone Global Library Limited
Picture research by Ruth Blair
Production by Victoria Fitzgerald
Originated by Capstone Global Library Ltd
Printed and bound in China by South China Printing Company Ltd

14 13 12 11 10
10 9 8 7 6 5 4 3 2 1

Library of Congress Cataloging-in-Publication Data

Ross, Stewart.
  World War I / Stewart Ross.
    p. cm. -- (Research it!)
  Includes bibliographical references and index.
  ISBN 978-1-4329-3494-1 (hc)
  1. World War, 1914-1918--Study and teaching--Handbooks, manuals, etc.--Juvenile literature. 2. Research--Handbooks, manuals, etc.--Juvenile literature. I. Title. II. Title: World War One. III. Title: World War 1.
  D522.4.R67 2009
  940.3072--dc22

  2009008756

Acknowledgments
The author and publishers are grateful to the following for permission to reproduce copyright material: Alamy: pp. **34** (©Photos 12), **30** (The Print Collector); The Art Archive: pp. **4** (Imperial War Museum), **31** (Eileen Tweedy); Bridgeman Art Library: p. **16** (The Illustrated London News Picture Library); Corbis: pp. **7, 9, 36** (Hulton-Deutsch Collection), **41** (Michael St. Maur Sheil), **24, 26**; Rex Features: pp. **46** (Roger-Viollet), **23, 39**; Stewart Ross: p.**42**; ©shutterstock and ©iStockphoto: background images and design features.

The main cover image, "Going over the top, Battle of the Somme, July 1, 1916", is reproduced with permission of ©The Art Archive/©Imperial War Museum. The background images are reproduced with the permission of the following: iStockphoto (©Olena Druzhynina, ©Boros Emese, ©Sascha Martynchuk) and shutterstock (©Gary Blakeley, ©Lars Lindblad, ©Picsfive, ©Theodore Scott, ©Michael Steden).

We would like to thank Rebecca Vickers for her invaluable help in the preparation of this book.

Every effort has been made to contact copyright holders of material reproduced in this book. Any omissions will be rectified in subsequent printings if notice is given to the publisher.

All the Internet addresses (URLs) given in this book were valid at the time of going to press. However, due to the dynamic nature of the Internet, some addresses may have changed, or sites may have changed or ceased to exist since publication. While the author and publisher regret any inconvenience this may cause readers, no responsibility for any such changes can be accepted by either the author or the publisher.

Contents

Some words are printed in bold, **like this**. You can find out
what they mean by looking in the glossary.

Why Research World War I?

Why do you carry out research? You carry out research because you want to know more about a subject. There are practical reasons for research, too. World War I changed the world forever. Indeed, World War II and the international political situation today cannot be properly understood without some knowledge of what happened between 1914 and 1918, when more than 8 million soldiers lost their lives.

You may feel that there has been so much careful investigation into a popular subject like World War I that there is no point in doing any more research. This misses the point of what history is. History is the study of past events—all past events. Each individual has a personal history, which is the story of his or her life. So, you could say that the history of the first day of a World War I battle like Verdun (February 21, 1916) is a blending of the histories—every second of every minute of every hour—of the hundreds of thousands of people involved. That's billions of tiny pieces of information—more than any historian could ever hope to master.

These British troops are in a front-line trench. The war involved so many millions of soldiers and civilians that a complete or definitive history of the war would be impossible to write.

The historical process

What historians do is select what seems the most important or relevant information, **interpret** it, and generalize about it. Each individual does this for himself or herself because no two people view the past in the same way.

Here are two examples of different views:

- A young British working-class woman might view U.S. participation in World War I as part of an economic struggle that did not concern the poor on either side. In contrast, an elderly German might see U.S. entry into World War I as an unnecessary development arising from the mistakes of the German leadership.
- Views change with time, too. Shortly after the Treaty of Versailles was signed (in 1919), many of the **Allies** saw it as just punishment for Germany. Later, the Versailles Treaty was seen as profoundly unwise because it was one of the elements that provoked World War II.

A KWL chart

A KWL chart shows us: What I <u>K</u>now, what I <u>W</u>ant to know, and what I <u>L</u>earned.

What I Know	What I Want to know	What I Learned
There has been a lot of historical work on World War I.	What is the point of my doing any more—surely all I have to do is read a book written by someone else?	Producing history is about selection, interpretation, and generalization. No two people will do this in the same way. So, if my research is competent and honest, my version of history will be as valid as another person's.

DEUTSCHE REICHSPOST.

What exactly is research?

1. The quest for evidence

The 5 Ws test

Who?
Who has produced the evidence?
Were they informed on the subject?

What?
What exactly is the evidence?
Is it original or a copy?

When?
When was it produced? Diaries and **memoirs** written after the war are generally less useful than those written at the time.

Where?
Where was it produced? A Russian newspaper report on the Russian Revolution of February 1917 will differ from one written in the United States.

Why?
Why was it produced? Is the evidence **propaganda** (see page 31), for example?

Like detectives, historical researchers work with **evidence**. This is information we gather when doing research. It allows us to piece together what happened in the past in order to understand events better. Generally, evidence can be divided into written evidence, usually known as a **source**, and visual, audible, or tangible (landscape, architecture, or artifact) evidence, such as a photograph or battlefield. Visual and audible evidence are also known as sources, but tangible evidence is normally not.

Not every piece of evidence is useful. To **evaluate** the usefulness of a piece of evidence, you can use the **5 Ws test** (see above).

SQ3R

A useful tool for handling written evidence is **SQ3R**:

Survey the **document**, scanning its contents to decide whether or not it will be of use.

Questions—What questions will the document answer as you read it carefully?

Read the document, taking notes.

Recall the key points of the document and see how they tie in with other research.

Review by rereading the document, checking your notes, and perhaps discussing with someone else what you have found.

2. Handling evidence

The four steps in handling evidence are generally:

- Find the evidence.
- Evaluate the evidence.
- Organize the evidence.
- Present the evidence.

This book will take you through the stages.

3. Objectivity

History is the search for truth. The researcher's duty is to remember this at all times. This is especially difficult when studying a war in which one's own country was involved, because we have been encouraged from birth to love, respect, and be proud of our country.

Primary and secondary sources

Historians distinguish between primary and secondary sources. Primary sources, such as letters and official documents, date from the time under examination. Secondary sources are accounts of events written by historians, journalists, and others.

Siegfried Sassoon (1886–1967)

Testing a primary source

Some primary sources are more useful than others. When consulting them, use the 5 Ws test. This example is based on the war poems of Siegfried Sassoon.

Who: Siegfried Sassoon was a wealthy, well-educated young writer from the British upper-middle class. He fought on the Western Front with exceptional bravery before becoming totally **disillusioned** with the war.

What: He wrote a series of deeply personal, bitter poems about the futility (hopelessness) of war.

When: His book *War Poems* was published in 1919.

Where: He fought on the Western Front.

Why: The poems were written to criticize the conduct of the war and war in general. When Sassoon published an attack on the war in 1917, the authorities said he was suffering from **"shell-shock"** (now recognized as post-traumatic stress disorder), and he was hospitalized.

Step 1: An Overview

For several reasons, World War I was unlike anything anyone had experienced before.

First, it was global. It did not begin that way. To start with, it was called the Great European War. However, even at this stage there was fighting in several continents and oceans as some of the major combatant nations—especially Great Britain, France, and Germany—had worldwide empires. **Imperial** rivalry carried the conflict into sub-Saharan Africa. Britain's alliance with Japan produced small-scale warfare in East Asia, and Anglo–German naval battles ensured that gunfire was heard in the Southern Hemisphere. Finally, the entry of the United States into the conflict in April 1917 ensured that what had started as a conflict in the **Balkans** (see page 17) had escalated into a genuine world war.

Second, the 1914–18 conflict was humankind's first experience of mechanized, industrialized warfare on a huge scale. Earlier wars—starting with the U.S. Civil War (1861–65)—had given clues to the future, but not until the barbed wire unrolled, the machine guns rattled, and the artillery thundered in 1914 did people realize the grim nature of modern warfare. Many individual soldiers came to see themselves as just numbers whose bravery or cowardice made little difference. What counted was the quantity of soldiers in the field and the firepower of the weapons made in factories back home.

Third, World War I was the first "**total war**." As we saw above, industry played as important a part in the outcome as the soldiers on the ground. Naval blockades and aerial bombing produced a civilian "home **front**" that paralleled the military one. **Conscription**, food rationing, and other hardships meant that the effect of the war was felt by a fighting nation's entire population. There was no escape. Indeed, when the fighting was over, many in the German military believed that they had been defeated by a collapse on the home front rather than the battle front.

Fourth, World War I was unique for the sheer horror of it. War is always terrible, but there had never been anything on this scale before: bodies blown apart by the hundreds, men gunned down in their thousands, battles lasting months, and in the end perhaps 13 million soldiers killed on the battlefields or dead from disease. No wonder, when it was all over, people spoke of it as the "war to end all wars."

The physical context

Geography provides the stage on which the drama of history is played out. As far as World War I is concerned, we particularly need to know:

1. Its political boundaries—for instance, just where was the place known as Austria-Hungary?
2. Certain physical features that influenced events, sometimes dramatically. The steep cliffs of the Gallipoli peninsula in the Dardanelles Strait (see map on page 10) are an example. Had those who planned the Allied invasion there in 1915 done their geography homework a bit more carefully, the campaign might have met with greater success.

These Allied invading forces are on the beaches of the Gallipoli peninsula in 1915. The failure of those who planned the Allied campaign to make allowances for the steep cliffs meant that the invaders were pinned down from the moment they landed. A little more geographic knowledge might have made all the difference.

Choosing and using maps

To find such information, we turn to maps.

What do we want to know?

As with all research, we need to have an idea, before we start, of what we are looking for. "Where World War I happened" is too vague for a realistic research target, so we need a list of the specific maps required. You can use the KWL tool to help.

- What we know: World War I was a global conflict fought largely in Europe.
- What we want to know: The detailed position of the main warring states and the major military campaigns.

This raises another issue. History is about change, and World War I lasted over four years. The physical shape of the world did not alter over that period, but plenty of boundaries and frontiers did. One single map, therefore, will not be enough.

This map shows the countries and empires of Europe in 1914, on the eve of World War I.

We might express our research targets as a diagram based upon the information given in the timeline. Note how it takes on an hourglass shape, starting with a world view, narrowing to specific battles, then broadening to a world view again:

Maps required

The world in June 1914: The political boundaries and major cities

⬇

Europe and the Middle East in June 1914: Countries and their **allegiances**

⬇

Areas of conflict: Western Front; Eastern Front; Eastern Mediterranean and Dardanelles; Middle East; Africa; Far East; oceans

⬇

Specific campaigns/battles, e.g., Tannenburg, 1914

⬇

Somme, 1916; Belleau Wood, 1918

⬇

The world in August 1918: Countries' allegiances and neutrality

⬇

The world in 1921: Countries and empires after the Versailles settlements

Note: This diagram assumes a military and political examination of the war. A different approach, focusing on its economic or social impact, would require different maps (which, incidentally, would be much harder to find).

Where to look for information

Here are four possible sources for the map information we require:

A general atlas

Advantages: An atlas is fine for the physical geography of the war, such as mountains and deserts. A good physical features map, for example, is essential to understanding the Arab revolt against the **Ottoman Empire**.
Disadvantages: It is not useful for political information, especially boundaries—for example, a modern map will show Poland, which did not exist as an independent country in 1914. Several place names have changed, too (see page 12).

The Internet

Advantages: The Internet has useful historical maps, but it is hard to locate and evaluate them. Google Earth is an exciting way to zero in on a physical feature that featured in the events of 1914–18. Try going to "Masurian Lakes," where the Russian army was defeated in September 1914, and see how difficult it must have been to maneuver an army in such tricky terrain.
Disadvantages: Most political and historical maps available for free lack detail and are often unreliable. It can be difficult to find what you need on one website. Physical geography maps on the Internet are of poor quality.

Names, languages, and dates

Be careful with place names and dates, especially in eastern Europe. You may come across the following problems.

Place names change

The best example is the Russian port of St. Petersburg. Before World War I, it was called St. Petersburg, like today. Since this sounded too German to the Russians, in 1914 it was changed to Petrograd. Between 1924 and 1991 it was Leningrad, in honor of the leader of the **Bolshevik** Revolution of 1917, Vladimir Ilyich Lenin.

Place names differ from language to language

Some changes are minor, such as the Austro-Hungarian "Triest" being "Trieste" in Italian. Others, such as "Gdańsk," are more confusing: during World War I this Baltic city was known by its German name, "Danzig."

Events in Russian history are often given with two dates

Before 1918 Russia used the old-style Julian calendar. Most of the rest of Europe had adopted the modern Gregorian calendar (which we still use today) by late in the 18th century. Therefore, the famous Bolshevik Revolution of 1917 is known as the "October Revolution" to the Russians. The rest of the world, using the Gregorian calendar, believed it started on November 7. On January 24, 1918 (Julian-style), Russia's new communist government switched to the Gregorian calendar. So, Wednesday, January 31, 1918, was followed by Thursday, February 14, 1918. Thousands of people in Russia missed their birthdays!

Books
Advantages: Maps in books are usually reliable. However, they are better for specific battles than for getting the bigger picture.
Disadvantages: Maps are in books to support the text, so they may not contain all the information you want.

A historical atlas
Advantages: A historical atlas is just what you need—an atlas containing maps produced by historians for historians, checked for accuracy, and covering every angle you could wish for.
Disadvantages: You may find a historical atlas too detailed.

Taking notes from maps
Taking notes from a historical atlas is not easy. Don't trace the maps. Ideally, you should decide which maps are relevant to your area of research and make your own rough sketch-map versions of them. This process involves:
1. reading/looking at words/images
2. registering in your mind what is being said
3. translating that information into your own sketch version on paper.

Going through this process guarantees that you digest and understand what you have read.

A KWL summary
Here is a summary in a KWL chart of what has been discussed in Step 1.

What I Know	What I Want to know	What I Learned
World War I was a global conflict fought largely in Europe	Detailed positions of the warring states and their campaigns	The political boundaries of 1914 and 1921, and the geography of the campaigns that led to these changes

Timeline of World War I

Timelines can be a useful resource in your research. In researching World War I, a timeline is particularly helpful in making it clear what was happening in different parts of the war at the same time.

Research areas

LTC = Long-Term Causes	IF = Italian Front
IC = Immediate Causes	OW = War in Ottoman Empire
WF1 = Western Front to end 1915	WA = War in the Air
WF2 = Western Front 1916–18	WS = War at Sea
EF = Eastern Front	PM = Peacemaking

14

Date	Event	Research area
1882	Italy joins Triple Alliance with Germany and Austria-Hungary, leaving France isolated within Europe.	LTC
1894	France and Russia sign military alliance.	LTC
1904	Britain and France draw closer with the *Entente Cordiale*. Military agreements follow. Russia joins the *Entente* three years later.	LTC
1911	Germany backs down and accepts French influence in Morocco.	LTC
June 28, 1914	A Bosnian terrorist group, backed by Serbia, assassinates Archduke Franz Ferdinand of Austria-Hungary.	IC
July 28, 1914	Austria-Hungary declares war on Serbia.	IC
Aug. 1, 1914	Germany declares war on Russia. France prepares for war.	IC
Aug. 4, 1914	The Allies (Britain, France, Belgium, Russia, and their empires and allies) are at war with the **Central Powers** (Germany, Austria-Hungary, and their empires and allies). German troops invade Belgium.	IC WF1
Aug. 14, 1914	First-ever bombing raid: French aircraft hit German airship hangars.	WA
Aug.–Sept. 1914	Germans smash advancing Russians at Tannenburg and Masurian Lakes.	EF
Sept. 1914	Battle of the Marne halts German advance on Paris. "Race to the Sea" produces trench warfare.	WF1
Nov. 1, 1914	Ottoman Empire joins war on the side of the Central Powers.	OW
Dec. 1914	Failure of French winter **offensive** confirms **attritional** nature of trench warfare.	WF1
Jan.–Feb. 1915	Germany introduces rationing and unrestricted submarine warfare (ends Sept 1915).	WS
April 1915	Combined forces of French, British, and **Anzacs** land on the Turkish Gallipoli peninsula, but fail to advance.	OW
April 26, 1915	Treaty of London: Italy joins Allies in return for Austrian territory. Italy attacks Austria in June.	IF

Date	Event	Research area
May 1915	Many thousands of Armenians are massacred by Turks in Asia Minor. Russians are driven back by massive Austro-Hungarian–German offensive. Germans attack at Ypres using poison gas.	OW WF1
May 31, 1915	First air raid on London by a Zeppelin airship.	WA
Sept. 1915	Failed French offensive in Artois region ends year of enormous casualties and neither side winning.	WF1
Feb. 21, 1916	Germans begin year-long assault on Verdun. Enormous casualties occur on both sides.	WF2
April 1916	Anglo-Indian force in Kut, **Mesopotamia**, surrenders to Turks. Britain's route to India is threatened.	OW
May 31, 1916	Battle of Jutland: British Royal Navy suffers heavy losses as it drives German High Seas Fleet into port.	WS
June–Sept. 1916	Russia's last great offensive grinds to a halt.	EF
July–Nov. 1916	Huge Anglo-French offensive on the Somme gains just 11 km (7 miles). Tanks first used in battle (Sept.).	WF2
Feb. 1, 1917	Germany infuriates United States by reintroducing unrestricted submarine warfare on merchant shipping. Allies adopt convoy system (May).	WS
Feb. 27, 1917	Order breaks down in Petrograd, leading to revolution and the abdication of Tsar Nicholas II in early March.	EF
March 1917	An Anglo-Indian force occupies Baghdad.	OW
April 1917	**Mutinies** occur in French Army.	WF2
April 6, 1917	Following intercepted "Zimmermann Telegram" and plea from President Woodrow Wilson, U.S. Congress declares war on Germany.	WF2
June–Nov. 1917	British capture Messines Ridge and launch another costly attritional offensive at Ypres.	WF2
Oct. 1917	Italians are defeated heavily at Battle of Caporetto.	IF
Oct. 24–25, 1917	Bolshevik-led Communist Revolution engulfs Russia.	EF
Dec. 1917	British and Arab forces take Jerusalem from Ottomans.	OW
Jan. 8, 1918	U.S. President Wilson sets out "14 Points" as a guideline for peacemaking.	PM
March 3, 1918	Treaty of Brest-Litovsk: Russia accepts harsh peace terms from Germany.	EF/PM
March–July 1918	Final German offensives fail to achieve breakthrough.	WF2
May 28, 1918	Cantigny: U.S. troops are in action for the first time.	WF2
July–Aug. 1918	Huge counterattack by Allies produces "Black Day of the German Army" (Aug. 8, 1918).	WF2
Sept.–Nov. 1918	U.S. St. Mihiel offensive and Allied Argonne-Meuse offensive are huge Allied advances that push Germans back.	WF2
Sept. 29, 1918	Bulgaria signs **armistice**, followed by Austria-Hungary on October 4.	EF/PM
Oct. 31, 1918	Turkish government accepts armistice.	OW/PM
Nov. 11, 1918	Germany agrees to armistice terms; war finally ends.	WF2/PM
June 28, 1919	Treaty of Versailles sets out harsh peace terms for Germany and establishes League of Nations. Further treaties deal with other defeated nations.	PM

Step 2: Researching the Basic Facts

Historians focus on three aspects of any event. We know these as the Three Cs: Causes, Course, and Consequences.

So, when we research the basic facts about World War I, we need to find out why it broke out, what occurred between August 4, 1914, and November 11, 1918, and what happened as a consequence of the war.

The Three Cs

Causes—Why did it happen?
Course—What happened?
Consequences—What were the results of the event's occurrence?

This image from the time shows military guards taking away Gavrilo Princip (shown by arrow), the assassin who killed Archduke Franz Ferdinand and his wife on June 28, 1914, in Sarajevo.

Causes

Trying to figure out the cause of events is difficult because it can involve blame ("Was the war anyone's fault?") and also deciding about how far back in time to go. For instance, Britain went to war because of a treaty it had made with Belgium in 1839; the reasons behind why it made this treaty could take us back to medieval times.

Long-term and short-term
Historians often distinguish between long-term and short-term causes:
1. Long-term causes cover the background to an event—how and why Europe became divided into two mutually hostile armed camps, for example.
2. Short-term causes are "triggers" that spark an event. The assassination of Archduke Franz Ferdinand of Austria on June 28, 1914, is an example.

Course

The "course" of events is the series of events that together make up World War I. Each of these events—such as the Russian Bolshevik Revolution of October/November 1917—has its own causes and consequences.

Consequences

Consequences are also controversial because they, too, can involve blame. They can also lead to debate about topics like the power of economics to shape history. Finally, they mean deciding how far forward in time to go—for instance, Germany's post-war **reparations** left the country vulnerable to the Great Depression, leading to the rise of the Nazis and World War II, which produced the Cold War . . . and so on.

Immediate, medium-term, and long-term
Historians often talk of immediate consequences and long-term consequences, and sometimes of medium-term consequences.
- The immediate consequences of World War I include, for example, the breakup of the **Austro-Hungarian Empire**. This was because countries declared independence from the empire even before the end of the war.
- A medium-term consequence of the war was Mussolini coming to power in Italy in 1922. This was because Italy's economy and government were weakened by the war. Many Italians decided Mussolini would be a strong leader who would make the country more stable and powerful.
- A long-term consequence was the emergence of the United States as the world's most powerful nation. This was because the war weakened the European empires, and the two world wars boosted the U.S. economy.

Where to start?

In their quest for basic information on a subject, most students turn first to the Internet and books. Let's examine each.

Free Internet sites

Let's assume you know almost nothing about World War I and you enter the phrase "World War I" into the search engine Ask.com. The first six listings might look something like this:

1. A request to narrow your search. 2. A link to Amazon.com. 3. A site about aircraft after World War I. 4. A vast multimedia history. 5. A site dealing only with the causes of the war. 6. A *Wikipedia* article on World War I.

If you need to know the basics of a subject, even the *Wikipedia* article presents serious problems:

- It is not written for school students, so it is often too complicated.
- There is no guarantee of its reliability because anyone can edit a *Wikipedia* article. There are editorial checks, but not by experts.
- Articles are often too long for basic research. For example, the entry on World War I is around 20,000 words.

Conclusion: An Internet search using a search engine is rarely the best way to begin research on a broad topic like World War I. A better way to start on the Internet would be to use an online research **database**. Most schools have access to some databases. Research databases are usually developed, and their information selected and checked for accuracy, for a specific audience, such as students of a particular grade level. Databases can have a wide range of sources, such as primary documents, newspapers, images, and encyclopedias. As databases are usually subscription services (where membership or payment is required), school and public libraries join on behalf of their users. Ask your teacher or a librarian what is available, how to use it, and for a user name and password.

An Internet website search

Advantages
An Internet search can be quick and easy, it is immediately appealing, there are tons of choices, and there is an almost infinite amount of information.

Disadvantages
There can be too much information to absorb, it is very hard to distinguish the valid site from the invalid, and there is no guarantee of a site's **objectivity**, accuracy, or comprehensiveness.

Books

Advantages: There are books written specifically for students; they are easy to take notes from and are likely to be accurate and easy to use.
Disadvantages: There are so many books that it is not easy to sort out what may be the most appropriate; if you have to buy them, nonfiction books can be expensive.

What book?

The next question is, which type of book makes the best starting point for research into World War I? There are three choices:

- Information books, such as Stewart Ross, *Timelines: World War I* (Mankato, Minn.: Smart Apple Media, 2007).
- Encyclopedias.
- Student encyclopedias. Since a book will probably be too detailed as a starting point, a student encyclopedia is probably the best bet. The advantages of these are that they are written at the appropriate level, they are brief and accurate, and they contain good links to further information.

Different encyclopedias

Encyclopedias vary widely, ranging from the massive adult version of the *Encyclopaedia Britannica* to a slender *Encarta*. They are available in book form or online: a book is easier to read and take notes from, but online versions are good for making links to other websites.

Beware!

- Make sure you select the encyclopedia that is best suited to your level. Try, for example, *World Book* online or in book form (the World War I article is about 9,400 words) or the more concise student edition of *Encyclopaedia Britannica*.
- Printing out an online encyclopedia's article is not research!

Bibliographies

A **bibliography** is a list of books used when producing a piece of work. The word is sometimes used to mean a recommended reading list. When it includes a variety of sources, such as movies and websites, it is generally known as a list of sources. Use bibliographies, reading lists, and lists of sources to find recommended material for further research. They are usually placed at the end of a book or article (see page 51).

Once you have chosen the article or book that best suits your needs, use the SQ3R technique (Survey, Question, Read, Recall, Review; see page 6) to take notes from it.

Step 3: Surveys and More Specialized Material

Now that we know the main facts of World War I and the main areas of controversy about the war, we are ready to choose a topic for our assignment.

Choosing an assignment topic

When choosing a topic for yourself, ask these questions:

- Am I really interested in this topic?
- Is there plenty of material on the subject?
- Is it the right size? A 1,000-word piece on the war at sea, for example, might be very difficult because there is so much information. On the other hand, you might not be able to find enough information in English for 1,000 words on gas warfare on the Eastern Front.
- Is the topic original? It is always more interesting to select a topic that has not been done many times before. For example, many U.S. students choose to write about the St. Mihiel Offensive, so it might be a good challenge to choose something less commonly explored.

If in any doubt, ask someone who will be able to help—a librarian or teacher.

Digging deeper

Filling in a KWL chart would be useful before starting. This one is on the Russian Revolution of 1917:

What I Know	What I Want to know	What I Learned
There were two revolutions in Russia in 1917—the first got rid of the czar and the second was the takeover by Bolshevik communists.	Why were there two revolutions?	Nothing yet—to be completed later

Listing sources

Most available secondary sources are in the form of books and the Internet. Of each we need to ask three questions:

Origin	Usefulness	Reliability	Appropriateness
Stewart Ross, *The Russian Revolution*, Chicago: Raintree, 2003	Subject divided into topic areas like "The Failure of the Provisional Government"	Experienced younger people's author	Language a bit difficult, but approach useful
en.wikipedia.org/wiki/Russian_Revolution_(1917)	Very long and quite adult, but has an excellent reading list at the end that includes primary sources	Author is mentioned, but there is a warning regarding citations	Maybe there are more appropriate sources?
www.worldbook.com/wb/article?idlar748536&stlrussian+revolution	Quite brief, but a useful introduction with subheadings	No author mentioned, no sources or reading list. Yet we have paid to access it—can it be trusted?	Language level about right and might make a useful starting point since facts can be cross-checked

A source examination

You can use the KWL method (see page 22) to judge the accuracy and usefulness of sources.

A very important lesson jumps out from this chart: when researching, a single source is never enough. By taking our information from more than one source, we can:

- acquire more information
- cross-check facts for accuracy
- learn about different interpretations of history.

What I **K**now	What I **W**ant to know	What I **L**earned
Russia's provisional government (1917) decided to continue fighting in the war.	Did the Russian people agree with this?	Nothing yet [see chart below]

Stewart Ross, in *The Russian Revolution*, says:
"The government felt bound to honor treaty obligations to foreign powers and ignored popular demands for peace." (p. 26)

On the other hand, the *World Book* website says:
"The new **soviet** . . . opposed the provisional government. . . . [It] claimed to represent the army and farm laborers as well as the town and city workers. Other soviets were set up throughout Russia. The soviets seriously restricted the government's ability to carry on the war with Germany, as many Russian army units refused to go on fighting."

In short, Ross says the Russian people wanted peace, while the *World Book* suggests that it was the communist Soviets that opposed the war. Perhaps both are right?

What has been learned from this exercise?

What I **K**now	What I **W**ant to know	What I **L**earned
Russia's provisional government (1917) decided to continue fighting in the war.	Did the Russian people agree with this?	It seems that most people wanted the war to stop, and the Soviets supported this wish.

You have also learned from looking closely at sources:

- to mistrust sources that are **anonymous**, vague (without specifics such as dates), and filled with generalizations
- that historical truth is sometimes impossible to find, especially when it comes to matters of sentiment (how people felt)
- that many answers are neither "yes" nor "no," but somewhere between the two.

Cutting-and-pasting

Cutting-and-pasting is a neat and simple computer shortcut method of moving text from one place to another—not so long ago a change meant typing the whole thing out again from scratch. However, cutting-and-pasting can lead to some very questionable—even illegal—research practices.

Here are three things you should *NEVER* do when cutting-and-pasting from your source to your research:

1. Never use it instead of taking notes.
2. Never use it to save writing your own text.
3. Never pass it off as your own work (this is **plagiarism**; see page 25).

This photograph shows Russian troops mutinying in 1917. A picture like this might suggest that the decision of the provisional government to continue fighting was a mistake.

Three note-taking methods

- Cut-and-pasted notes from the *World Book* website on the history of tanks might look this:

  Tanks . . . name from the British . . . developed them during World War I (1914– 1918) . . . called them water tanks to conceal their purpose . . . first used tanks against the Germans in the Battle of the Somme in 1916 . . . slow and clumsy . . . used successfully in the Battle of Cambrai in 1917.

  This extract is too long (47 words from the original 66), poorly laid out, and has not helped you to remember the content.

- Here are some cut-and-pasted notes assembled from the *Wikipedia* entry on the history of tanks:

  Tank or "landship" development was sponsored by the First Lord of the Admiralty, Winston Churchill. It culminated in the Mark I tank prototype, named Mother. The first tank in battle was designated D I, a British Mark I, during the Battle of Flers-Courcellette on September 15, 1916. Germany fielded very few tanks during World War I.

  If these notes are used as part of a written assignment, any teacher will be able to spot that this sort of writing is almost certainly not a student's. Even more seriously, you are guilty of plagiarism.

- In contrast, this conventional note-card method (below right) has 26 words, and it is clear, concise, and memorable (because it uses your own words—for example, "secret").

This dramatic photo of a British Mark IV tank was probably staged. Although big and impressive-looking, British tanks were often less effective than the smaller, turreted French models.

Tanks in WWI
- *Brit invention*
- *name from water tanks (secret)*
- *slow & clumsy*
- *used vs. Germans (1) Battle Somme (1916): unsuccessful; (2) Battle Cambrai (1917): successful.*

Plagiarism

Plagiarism is passing off someone else's work as your own. It is using other people's work and words without admitting that you are doing so. This is not always against the law, but it is dishonest and morally wrong. Moreover, if discovered it will probably lead to your work being given the lowest possible grade. You might even fail the class or be expelled from your school. Plagiarism is nearly always obvious to an experienced teacher for the following reasons:

- The written style will differ from a student's other work, perhaps even changing during the course of a piece of writing. A U.S. student may suddenly start using British spelling, for instance.
- The same piece of plagiarized text—for example, from *Wikipedia*—may find its way into the answer of more than one student.
- The sources of plagiarized text are often highly unoriginal.
- Students in a hurry frequently plagiarize text that is approximately—but not exactly—what is required. The result is writing and information that is inappropriate, off the subject, or irrelevant.
- Students who plagiarize often use poor and inaccurate sources, such as personal or non-academic websites.
- Plagiarized text may be at a different intellectual level—usually higher—than the text around it.
- Many teachers use an online plagiarism detector.

Plagiarism is cheating and does not help your intellectual or academic progress.

Taking and organizing notes

Taking notes from a source has four functions:

1. It gives you a neat summary of facts and ideas.
2. It makes you read a text carefully and understand it—you can't take useful notes on something you don't understand.
3. It helps you remember information because notes are processed by your brain. This does not happen when you just read or cut-and-paste.
4. It enables you to organize information quickly and easily.

Example:

Researching U-boats for your assignment on "The War at Sea, 1914–18," you come across this text on the *World Book* site:

During World War I (1914–1918), Germany proved the submarine's effectiveness as a deadly warship. In 1914, the German submarine U-9 sank three British cruisers within an hour. German submarines, called Unterseeboote or U-boats, blockaded the United Kingdom and took a heavy toll of merchant and passenger ships. U-boats became the terror of the seas by waging unrestricted war on Allied ships.

In May 1915, a German submarine torpedoed the British liner Lusitania. The attack killed 1,201 passengers, including 128 Americans. Public anger increased in the United States as U-boats sank one American merchant ship after another during the next year. These submarine attacks helped lead to the entry of the United States into the war in April 1917.

To take notes from these paragraphs:
- Read the full text.
- Read the text again, thinking about the main points it is making.
- Read it a third time, underlining or highlighting key information.
- Write down the marked words clearly and concisely. Use abbreviations (for example, "U.S." for United States, "sub" for submarine), numbers, bullet points, underlining, headings and subheadings, plenty of paragraphs and colors, and avoid unnecessary words, such as articles (for example, "a German submarine" might become "German sub").
- Check your notes against the original text to make sure they match up.

Subs in WWI (1914–18)
- Germany proved its effectiveness—subs called Unterseeboote (U-boats).
- Deadly—e.g., (1914) U-9 sank 3 Br cruisers in 1 hr.
- Blockaded GB, sinking merchant and passenger ships.
- "Terror of the seas" with unrestricted war on Allied ships—e.g., May 1915 U-boat torpedoed Br liner Lusitania: 1,201 passengers killed, inc. 128 Americans.
- Sinking of many U.S. ships increased public anger (i.e., anti-German) & helped U.S. entry into war, April 1917.

This photograph shows the sinking of the Italian steamer Stromboli by a German U-boat in 1917.

SQ3R—The Battle of Jutland (1916)

In deciding whether a source is suitable for your research, the SQ3R tool might be useful. For example, researching "The War at Sea, 1914–18," in the library you come across an interesting-looking book: Andrew Gordon's *The Rules of the Games: Jutland and British Naval Command* (Annapolis, Md.: Naval Institute, 1996). Is it useful?

Survey
A quick flip through reveals it is a fascinating and scholarly book (with some great action pictures!), but it is very detailed and the chapter headings seem confusing—for example, "The Long Calm Lee of Trafalgar." Conclusion: Proceed with caution.

Question
Gordon gets down to the war only about halfway through. Your specific research question is, "What was the importance of the Battle of Jutland (1916)?" You do not have time to read the whole book. As a shortcut, go to the final chapter ("Perspective").

Tip: Most authors provide a summary of their work at the end of the book.

Read
The first three pages of the last chapter give us the key information we need:

- Both sides claimed victory at Jutland.
- The British fleet lost three battle cruisers to the German fleet's one.
- The British fleet lost 10 percent of its men in casualties, the Germans 6 percent.
- The German fleet retired, leaving the British Royal Navy in control of the surface of the seas.
- The battle showed serious weaknesses in the Royal Navy's ship design and ways of thinking.

Recall
This information is easily remembered and fits in well with what you know about the German U-boat (submarine) campaign.

Review
What we have learned supports the idea that World War I was not decided only on the battlefield, but also in the shipping lanes. Britain, France, and the United States gradually depleted Germany's resources by cutting its supply lines.

Specialized material based on original sources can be fascinating and gives a real insight into the subject under research. However, it is often longer than you need, too detailed, and difficult to read—so be careful!

Step 4: Newspapers

Accessible primary sources

As explained on page 7, primary sources provide actual historical facts that have not been processed by a historian. The Internet has made newspapers the most accessible written primary source. Copies of nearly all the major newspapers can be viewed online, although some demand a fee to use their **archive** service.

Here are two useful newspaper archive sites:
- *New York Times:* www.nytimes.com/ref/membercenter/nytarchive.htm. It's quite easy to use and its advanced search is useful. However, to access some of the articles, you have to pay.
- *The Times* (London): http://archive.timesonline.co.uk/tol/archive. It takes time to get the hang of using it and it requires payment.

Example of newspaper research

These two newspaper accounts examine the mood in the United States and Britain at the start of 1918.

The *New York Times* is full of the role the United States is expected to play in the year ahead: "Confidence in America is great among the hard-pressed European allies, both for moral and material reasons." The writer speaks of "the profound necessity of peace" and how the war will bring in "a period of freedom, justice and security." In short, the mood as reflected in the paper is one of optimism.

The Times of London is more mixed. The news from the battle fronts appears good, with many reports of successes. Yet there are huge casualty lists and a massive advertisement—headed "Ships! Ships! Ships!"— announcing that more merchant ships urgently need to be built. The writer announces grimly, "The whole civilized world must look forward with awe to the year which opens today." And on the same page an article announces sternly, "there is none too young, or too old, or too feeble to play his or her part." Clearly, London did not share New York's optimism.

Because of **censorship**, newspapers are probably more helpful for research into the home front than the battle front. The articles, language, pictures, and advertisements offer us a special window into the past.

Newspapers: Strengths and weakness

Strengths

- You get a broad cross-section/slice of life at the time, from politics to business and sports.
- You can get precise detail of events.
- They are easy to access and read.
- As businesses, newspapers had to reflect the needs of their readers—this opens windows into the minds of those people.

Weaknesses

- Under the pressure of time, newspaper editors may have gotten some of their facts wrong.
- Some articles contain personal opinions that may not be shared by others.
- They may give an image of only one section of society: the readers. *The Times*, for instance, was the mouthpiece of the educated upper and upper-middle classes. Its casualty lists mentioned only officers.

To evaluate the usefulness and reliability of a newspaper article, we need to apply the "5 Ws" test: Who, What, When, Where, Why?

Here is a piece from the *New York Times* of May 18, 1918:

CHEERED BY BRITISH ON ARRIVAL

WITH THE AMERICAN ARMY IN FRANCE, May 17, (Associated Press.) – Troops of the new American army within the British zone in Northern France are completing their training in the area occupied by troops which are blocking the path of the Germans to the Channel ports. Their commander has already commanded American forces in trenches on the French front.

The British officers and men who are training the new force say that the Americans are of the finest material and are certain to give a most excellent account of themselves when they meet the Germans.

Who?
The piece is anonymous . . . might a U.S. officer have written it for a reporter?

These U.S. soldiers are entering the town of Nonsard in France in 1918. The presence of hundreds of thousands of fresh U.S. troops on the Western Front, commanded by General John Pershing, helped to change the course of the war.

What?

We are given almost no detail. All we know is:

1. Some U.S. forces have arrived in the British zone in northern France.
2. They are being trained by the British.
3. They are led by a U.S. officer with experience in trench warfare.
4. The two armies appear to get along well.
5. Some incidental material is provided, such as the fact that the German army was aiming at the Channel ports.

When? and Where?

May 17, 1918. Written in northern France, which is a huge area.

Why?

The piece was not written to give the reader facts. Information such as the number of troops and their position would have been reported back immediately to the enemy. Instead, the article has a "feel-good" purpose. The mood is optimistic, making Americans feel that they were right to enter the war. The position they are in is crucial, the men are admirable—this is all positive propaganda. Obviously, an article such as this has to be read alongside other sources in order to get a broader, fairer picture. On its own, it is simply propaganda.

Here is an example of positive propaganda from *The Times* on July 3, 1916, reporting the first day of the Battle of the Somme (July 1, 1916):

> ## BRITISH HEADQUARTERS, SATURDAY
> At half-past 7 this morning a great battle began on a front of about 5 miles above and on both banks of the Somme . . . I will only say . . . that at the first assault we over-ran the enemy's front line almost everywhere and in places are now well within his territory.

It is now known that the first day of the Battle of the Somme was, in fact, the most disastrous in terms of casualties in the history of the British Army.

Propaganda

Propaganda is subjective material, such as words and images, produced to support a particular point of view. It can be positive, praising the successes and good qualities of one's own side, or negative, attacking the enemy.

During World War I, all countries used propaganda extensively. The most extreme form of propaganda is called black propaganda—material produced by one side to look as if it has come from the other.

Tip: Try hard to identify propaganda by not taking any information at its face value.

This positive propaganda poster was used to gain support for Liberty Bonds. These were war bonds sold by the U.S. government to raise money to support the Allies in World War I.

Step 5: Documents

What is a document?

A document is any piece of paper with writing on it. Historians commonly use the term to mean a primary source of no more than a few pages. For the best research, this should be in its original form and not typeset and then printed because:

- Mistakes can creep in when documents are typed out.
- Tiny details—such as the type of paper, handwriting, and crossings out—can be useful clues to the researcher.
- Printing often means selection—another historian has decided what is worth reproducing. That decision may not have been wise.

It is unusual, however, for students to get their hands on original documents (except those in the family), so they have to make do with photocopies or typeset versions.

Types of original document

These are some of the original documents of use to those researching World War I:

- statistics, such as names and numbers of men in a unit and casualty lists
- financial records, such as bills
- laws
- written notes, messages, and orders
- **verbatim** reports of speeches
- official military reports, such as battle reports and the proceedings of court martials (military courts that try people in the armed forces according to military law)
- letters
- diaries
- newspapers
- autobiographies
- poetry and other literature.

This list is in order of overall factual reliability, although not everyone would agree with this ordering.

Problems with original documents

Number

An individual could not possibly master all the documents relating to, for example, the U.S. Army, let alone those of the other combatant nations. Historians overcome this by (1) selecting documents felt to be representative, and (2) combining their work with that of others.

Reliability

"Reliability" is a difficult concept. Here are two examples:

- A casualty list is reliable in one way—assuming it is correct, it tells us precisely how many men were put out of action at a specific time. It does not tell us (a) how they were killed and injured, (b) the significance of the loss (did it bring a great victory or was it a terrible waste?), or (c) the effect of the casualties on morale.
- An autobiography is in one sense a wholly reliable document: it says precisely what the author remembers or thinks he or she remembers. But this gives us the experiences, thoughts, and memories of one individual. Different people have totally different experiences and remember them in different ways.

Documents and interpretation

Documents become valuable only when a historian uses them to throw light on the past. We call this process interpretation.

Here is an extract from the Treaty of Versailles, signed on June 28, 1919—it is the peace settlement that followed World War I:

Article 42. Germany is forbidden to maintain or construct any fortifications either on the left bank of the Rhine or on the right bank to the west of a line drawn 50 kilometers [31 miles] to the East of the Rhine . . .

Article 45. As compensation for the destruction of the coal mines in the north of France and as part payment towards the total reparation due from Germany for the damage resulting from the war, Germany cedes to France in full and absolute possession, with exclusive right of exploitation, unencumbered and free from all debts and charges of any kind, the coal mines situated in the Saar Basin . . .

A historian might interpret this document this way:

"Since Versailles was drawn up by the Allies, it tells us about their thinking, not the Germans. Both of these clauses tell Germany what to do: this does not suggest a normal, agreement-style treaty. Because the treaty was signed on the anniversary of the assassination of Archduke Franz Ferdinand of Austria, the event that sparked the war, it was probably designed finally to end what had begun five years before.

"Signing the treaty in the Palace of Versailles, where the German Empire had been declared in 1871, suggests a desire to humiliate the defeated. Finally, why was the treaty so one-sided? The impression we get is of a thirst for revenge on the part of those who dictated it. But we do not know whether this was their aim, or whether they were following the wishes of the wider public."

The signing of what came to be known as the Treaty of Versailles took place at the Palace of Versailles outside Paris on June 28, 1919.

The literature of World War I

Among the best-known documents from the era of World War I is the poem "Dulce et Decorum Est" by the young soldier-poet Wilfrid Owen. Here are some extracts from it:

> Bent double, like old beggars under sacks,
> Knock-kneed, coughing like hags, we cursed through sludge . . .
> . . . Gas! Gas! Quick, boys!—An ecstasy of fumbling,
> Fitting the clumsy helmets just in time;
> But someone still was yelling out and stumbling
> And flound'ring like a man in fire or lime . . .
> Dim, through the misty panes and thick green light,
> As under a green sea, I saw him drowning . . .
>
> If you could hear, at every jolt, the blood
> Come gargling from the froth-corrupted lungs,
> Obscene as cancer, bitter as the cud
> Of vile, incurable sores on innocent tongues,—
> My friend, you would not tell with such high zest
> To children ardent for some desperate glory,
> The old Lie: Dulce et decorum est
> Pro patria mori.*
>
> *Latin for "It is sweet and right to die for your country"

Because works like this are so powerful, they present the researcher with problems:
- Much wartime literature is in some way antiwar.
- It is widely read by those who do not study history.
- The popular images of World War I are of foul and muddy trenches, generals encouraging men to join the army, and rows of gravestones.
- Therefore, the poetry is taken to reinforce a popular impression of the war as horrible, pointless, and deeply unpopular.

What could the researcher's response to these problems be?
- All wars are horrible. The principal difference between World War I and other wars was the scale of the slaughter.
- Pointless? There are certainly arguments on both sides.
- Most historians say that the participants saw the war as tragic, but it was not deeply unpopular. Among British soldiers (Owen was British), only three small, serious mutinies were reported.

So, be wary of using literary documents as historical sources. They may support or illustrate other evidence, but never use them as a source on their own.

Step 6: Images

World War I was the first major conflict to be photographed extensively, the first to be filmed, and the first to be painted by numerous official war artists. As a result, we have more images of it than of all previous wars put together. The result is a wonderful resource for researchers, but one that must be handled carefully. This is partly because there is so much material and partly because images are tricky pieces of historical evidence.

Types of image

Film

All the film taken at the battle fronts was official. For reasons of morale, it tends not to show the more horrifying aspects of war and concentrates on advance rather than retreat. That said, real film footage of real battles shocked many of those at home. The classic example is the British film *Somme*, part of which can be viewed on www.iwm.org.uk/server/show/nav.00o003004004. (See also page 38.)

Example: In Flanders Fields

This photo provides detailed information about war on the Western Front:
- It shows the nature of this specific piece of terrain.
- You can see the British Army uniforms.
- It shows the type of stretcher.
- It took a number of men (at least four) to carry one wounded soldier.

You can give the photo the 5 Ws test:

What can we learn from this photo?

Photos

When searching through the thousands of World War I photographs, ask yourself, "Who took this picture and why?" Also, try not to concentrate just on the grisly battlefield images. Look also at the less well-known, but equally informative, shots of soldiers at rest, of factories and workers, and of ships and civilian streets.

Who took the photo? We don't know from the image itself.

What does it show? British stretcher-bearers carrying a wounded or dead colleague over churned up and flooded terrain on the Western Front.

When was it taken? Sometime during the winter months of 1916-17, probably. Even if we had a descriptive caption, how could we guarantee its reliability?

Where? Again, without a reliable caption we can say only that the picture was taken on the British sector of the Western Front. It might even have been staged elsewhere. Who knows what was going on behind the camera?

Why? There are many unanswered questions: Did the photographer suddenly come across this scene and decide to take it? Was the picture posed, possibly with actors? Did the photographer choose the muddiest piece of the battlefield, or was the scene typical of conditions everywhere?

Conclusion:

The photograph offers some detailed *factual* information and a great deal of *emotional* information. The terrible blasted landscape, the posture of most of the men, the depth of mud, the body on the stretcher, the misty horizon, the water, the dismal, depressing feel of the whole scene—all of these factors strike us forcibly.

The powerful emotional impact of such an image can lead the researcher into unwise generalization. We read reports that the battlefield was churned up by shell fire, then look at the photograph—and imagine all the battlefields were like this. We read depressing poems like Wilfrid Owen's (see page 35), and we imagine all soldiers were constantly struggling their way through mud, like those in the photo.

Finally, remember that the photographs chosen to illustrate books are usually selected to have the maximum impact. Priority is given to the shocking, grisly, and eye-catching. Images illustrate conclusions and give them emotional force. They are often less reliable as sources.

Tip: Don't generalize from images. It is unwise to reach broad conclusions based on a single photograph or even from a set of photographs.

Artwork

Artwork includes paintings, sketches, cartoons, and posters. Most of it was official—unofficial painting or drawing at the front was censored in case it assisted the enemy. Even more than a photograph, a painting or drawing is a piece of creative work that captures emotion as well as fact. As with photos, ask yourself, "Who produced this picture and why? Is it an objective source of factual historical information?"

Can the camera lie?

The camera can lie and can't lie.
- It can't lie because it can reproduce only what is before it when the shutter is open.
- It can lie because (1) the subject of the picture can be posed or staged to give a false impression and (2) photographic prints can be altered.

The British film *Somme* (see URL on page 36) is a good example of staged photography. In the film, the figure shown being shot as he leaves the trench is clearly acting! Altering photographs after they were taken was still rare, although there is a famous example from shortly after the war.

Copyright

Be aware of copyright laws when including images in written assignments. Students may normally reproduce pictures from the Internet and other sources if they are purely for personal research or part of a project for school. However, check a photograph's "terms of use" (often through an Internet link). While some sites allow free use, others do not.

Written out of history

Following the communist takeover at the end of 1917, Russia plunged into a bitter and bloody civil war. There were divisions, too, within the ruling group of Bolsheviks. Who, for example, should take over after the death of Lenin, the man who had engineered the Communist Revolution? One answer was Leon Trotsky, shown in this 1920 photo on page 39, standing at the base of a platform from which Lenin was speaking.

Eventually Lenin was replaced not by Trotsky, but by Josef Stalin. The disgraced Trotsky fled into exile and was later murdered by Stalin's agents. Within the Soviet Union, all written and pictorial traces of Trotsky were removed.

Handling images

"A picture," so the proverb says, "is worth a thousand words." This implies that an image combines information and emotion in a single, powerful, and easily understandable form. For gathering detailed information, it is wonderful; as a source of understanding, however, it is much less reliable.

Here Lenin, the Soviet communist leader, addresses a crowd in 1920. The figure outlined in red is Leon Trotsky, thought at the time to be a possible successor to Lenin. When Josef Stalin, not Trotsky, took over as leader of the Soviet Union, Stalin had the image of his rival removed from the photo.

Step 7: Other Evidence

One of the most interesting sources of information about World War I is physical, tangible evidence. This ranges from human-made objects, such as a rifle, to architecture and even whole battlefields. The trouble with this sort of evidence is that much of it is not readily available, especially to students living outside Europe. There are, however, museums all over the world containing exhibits from World War I.

Types of tangible evidence

Here is a list of some of the more accessible forms of tangible evidence:

- Military equipment: This ranges from bullets to machine guns, uniforms, cooking utensils, and backpacks.
- Machinery: This includes the big objects like tanks, armored cars, and heavy guns, and smaller things like bicycles.
- Domestic articles: Any household artifact, such as a washbasin or candle holder, helps build up a picture of the period.
- Graves and memorials: These include anything from a single grave to huge cemeteries.
- Trenches and other structures: The landscape around where the battles were fought is still littered with the remains of trenches, **bunkers**, and other fortifications.
- Landscape: Although the landscape has changed over the last century, the basic pattern of hills, valleys, rivers, and plains remains the same.

Using tangible evidence

Tangible evidence rarely helps to directly answer broad, sweeping questions, such as, "Why did the war break out?" or "What were its consequences?" Indeed, a number of academic historians show no interest at all in tangible objects. They concentrate instead on documentary evidence.

On the other hand, tangible evidence has many uses:

1. It enables the researcher to get the "feel" of a period of history. Putting on a gas mask, for instance, can help one understand the panic a soldier felt when a gas attack was expected. Stand in front of a massive World War I tank, such as the Mark IV pictured on page 24, and imagine how you would feel if, never having seen one before, you suddenly found that steel monster clanking toward you.

These tracks cross an area where part of the Battle of the Somme was fought over six months in 1916. Only 11 kilometers (7 miles) of ground was gained by the Allies during the Somme campaign, at the total cost of over a million casualties on all sides.

2. It allows us to understand why the war took the form it did. Looking at a massive German bunker near Verdun, for example, one can begin to understand why defense dominated attack for much of the war.

3. The gigantic battlefield war cemeteries and the architecture around them bring home the scale of the slaughter and just how much that meant to those who survived.

4. Why a battle turned out as it did can sometimes be fully understood only by going to the place itself. Driving through the battlefield areas of Belgium and northern France and noting the network of streams, rivers, and canals, one can start to imagine what happened to the landscape when artillery fire smashed the banks, channels, locks, and so on.

WARNING: Exploring World War I battlefields is extremely dangerous because of unexploded munitions. It is estimated that buried in the ground around Verdun alone there remain 12 million unexploded shells.

Oral evidence

Almost all important recorded evidence has also been written down, so what does hearing an actual voice from the period bring to your research? It gives a sense of authenticity and an insight into the culture of the era that is not possible from the written word alone.

There are few sound recordings from the era of World War I. Film was still silent and magnetic tape had yet to be invented. Sound recording was made onto a disc of soft material, such as wax, and the heavy apparatus was not easily portable. Sound recordings that might interest students researching World War I include:

Political speeches

Listen to the vocabulary (more difficult than today), the accents, and the formality of the world's leaders in recorded political speeches. Recordings of President Woodrow Wilson and others can be heard at http://memory.loc.gov/ammem/nfhtml/.

Popular songs

Words on their own are powerful, but words with music can be stronger. We can truly appreciate the power of most World War I songs only by hearing them with music; try www.firstworldwar.com/audio/itsalongwaytotipperary.htm.

This is the British war cemetery at Etaples, France. A visit to a cemetery like this brings home to the researcher, far more powerfully than statistics, the enormous scale of the slaughter that marked World War I.

Soldiers' songs

Soldiers' songs offer an insight into the soldiers' minds. But be careful! Many of them contain very strong language.

Postwar interviews with soldiers who had fought in World War I

Postwar interviews with soldiers are interesting because of the way the veterans recall the past. They are a lot more matter-of-fact than one would expect. Is that memory blunting their emotions, or do we dramatize and even romanticize the war experience?

Interviews with those who remember talking with war veterans

Interviews with non-soldiers who talked to veterans is the least reliable but most accessible source. Soldiers may have had children in the 1920s—and you will be able to interview those people about what their fathers told them (if anything) about World War I.

Battlefields and cemeteries

Europe is littered with World War I battlefields and memorials—too many to be listed here. To English-speakers, the best known and most accessible are in France and Belgium, where the enormous cemeteries never fail to stun visitors. Some of these sites have small museums nearby—for example, at Albert, France. Other countries also have national cemeteries and memorials to the dead of World War I. What follows is just a small selection.

ANZAC War Memorial, Darwin, Australia
Arlington National Cemetery, Arlington, Virginia, United States
British Empire Cemetery, Etaples, France
Canadian National Memorial, Vimy, France
Canterbury Cemetery, Gallipoli, Turkey
Cenotaph, Ottawa, Canada
Cenotaph, Wellington, New Zealand
Gorlice War Cemetery, Gorlice, Poland
Hunkovce Cemetery, Slovakia
Köln German Cemetery, Nordrhein, Westfalen, Germany
Mărăti Mausoleum, Romania
Memorial Museum, Passchendaele, Belgium
Pocol War Cemetery, Pocol, Italy
Sanctuary Wood Trench Museum, Ypres, Belgium
South African National Memorial, Delville Wood, Somme, France
Verdun Memorial, Verdun, France

For a more comprehensive list of World War I cemeteries, see www. ww1cemeteries.com/ww1cemeteries/othercemeteriesandmemorials.htm.

Step 8: Your Viewpoint

Thinking over research

After assembling your evidence, you need to stand back and think about it, turning it over in your mind and asking questions about it. Ideally, this process should take a day or two.

Ask yourself the following questions:

- Why did you choose the topic? Has your research justified your choice?
- What ideas or concepts did you have before you started? How have these been changed by what you have discovered?
- What have other writers said about your topic? Do you agree with them?
- In general terms, what are the conclusions of your research?
- Have you uncovered anything new and original? Be careful: you are unlikely to be in a position to challenge professional historians. One area where you might contribute something genuinely new is on a very specific topic, such as the impact of the war on people from your town or city.

Having gone through this process in your mind, you need to start setting out the results of your research.

Types of presentation

We will assume that the topic of our research has been the weaponry of the Western Front. Essentially, there are two ways to present the results of research:

- Handbook-type research: Produce a sort of information package or handbook. This goes through the main categories of weaponry—such as small arms, mortars, artillery, gas, and tanks—and discusses the main features of each.
- Question-type research: Use the same information to answer a question, such as, "Which side had the more effective weaponry on the Western Front?" This approach is more difficult, but will probably produce a more interesting paper.

Defining your topic

Before going any further, it is necessary to define the limits of your topic. For example, while researching weaponry, you may have included aircraft. But would this extend to airships? To keep a tight focus, you might limit yourself to land weapons.

Structuring and organizing notes

It is unlikely that notes from different sources will be structured in the right way for a paper. They need reorganizing.

If we are writing a handbook-type paper, the notes relating to individual weapons need to be brought together. This can be done by writing them out, grouping all the notes on machine gun, rifle, cannon, and so on together, or it can be more easily done by underlining or highlighting with different colors. For example, you may highlight all your references to rifles in green, to machine guns in yellow, to artillery in red, and so on.

Writing a question–type paper involves the same technique, but underlining or highlighting different topics. For example, if your question is "How important was gas as a weapon on the Western Front?" then you might highlight references to the power of gas as a weapon in red and its drawbacks in yellow.

Tip: The methods suggested here may work for most students, but in the end it is up to individuals to figure out which they prefer. All that matters is that you organize your notes properly. Confusing notes reflect confused thoughts and usually lead to a confusing final paper.

Concept web

The concept web is an excellent way to start to organize a subject. Begin by putting the main topic in the center of a piece of paper, then subheadings on lines branching out from it and other ideas branching out from the subheadings, like the one below on weaponry.

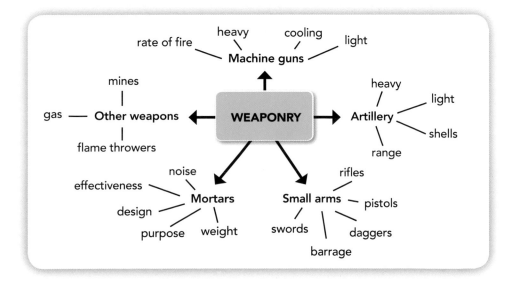

Ways to develop a viewpoint

Why

The next step is to decide what argument you are going to make. Failure to do this will mean:

1. Your paper will be dull because it lacks a point of view. It will read like a train schedule.
2. Worse still, you may change your mind midway through your paper, destroying its credibility.

How

In a handbook-type paper, introduce:

- Comparison: For example, when discussing the French Renault FT tank, you might compare it to the larger, yet more cumbersome, British tanks.
- Judgment: For example, you may conclude that the Renault tank's turret gave it a more flexible weapon than the British Mark IVs and Vs.

This photo shows French Renault tanks in action in 1918. For narrow patriotic reasons, some British books make little mention of these highly effective weapons.

Questions have answers

In a question-type paper, there is no difficulty developing a viewpoint. This is because you will have to make comparisons and judgments in order to answer the question. The only problems for the researcher are being consistent and objective (see below).

Objectivity

As soon as history ceases to be objective, it ceases to be history—it is simply propaganda, myth, or fairy tale. Objectivity is judging rationally using undisputed evidence. Lack of reliable facts makes perfect objectivity impossible. However, good historical researchers try to:

- Set aside preconceptions. For example, the British popular media can give the impression that British troops were holding the Western Front together from the winter of 1916 onward. Yet it was French forces that saved the Allies from disaster during the German attacks of spring 1918.
- Go where your research takes you, no matter how unwelcome the path. Remember that you are aiming to uncover the true story of what happened. War is complicated, and you won't always like what you find.
- Belong to no nation or race—the most difficult exercise of all. Students want their people to have done great things. Germans emphasize how they were never defeated; the British claim to have saved France (and even Europe) by joining the war; Americans believe their intervention brought an Allied victory. All of these claims are to some extent true. In the end, though, do they matter? The war is long finished. What we need now is cool reflection, not nationalistic boasting.
- Judge by the standards of the day, not those of the present. For instance, you will disagree with the widespread racism in the United States at the time of World War I. But historians do not condemn the past for not being like the present. They may note that the U.S. Army had all-black regiments, but it is not their job to say that things *should* have been otherwise.

Step 9: Presentation

The last crucial stage of your project is how to present it most effectively. We will assume that the research topic has been the causes of World War I.

As already seen (page 44), there are two written ways of presenting our research:

1. A handbook-type, such as a year-by-year account of events that led up to August 1914, with a summary at the end. This format is more story than analysis.
2. A question-type paper, such as "Why did World War I break out?" or, "Could World War I have been prevented?"

Answering a question

For this example, your question is: Why did World War I break out in 1914?

Basic structure

All answers divide into three basic sections:

1. *Introduction*: This sets out the intentions of your paper and how you will be addressing it.
2. *Evidence and argument*: This contains the bulk of your answer, putting forward evidence and exploring possible different answers.
3. *Conclusion*: This sums up your conclusion based on all that has gone before.

Plan

Writing a plan is like consulting a map before setting out on a journey—you need to know where you are going. Within the three-part basic structure (above), divide the plan into paragraphs and link each paragraph to your notes. Some people use numbers or colors to do this.

Writing your paper

After all the careful preparation, the actual writing of your paper should not be too difficult. Here are some guidelines:

Answer the question

Continually ask yourself: Is this relevant? How is it answering the question? Try to relate directly back to the question at least once on every page.

Example of a plan for a written assignment

Remember, this plan is just an example. There are—literally—dozens of ways to structure a paper on the causes of World War I. You might try organizing your assignment like this:

Para 1
Introduction: Quote Keegan (my notes page 3). Reasons for war very complex (my notes p. 1) and controversial (my notes p. 8). My thesis: war not inevitable but result of mistakes of judgment taken at key moments.

Para 2
Long-term causes: (a) French humiliation in war of 1870–71 (notes p. 3)—Alsace and Lorraine & thirst for revenge. Isolation then Treaty with Russia (notes p. 3) and Entente with GB (notes p. 6).

Para 3
Long-term causes (continued): (b) Construction of Triple Alliance (notes p. 2)—concept of 2 armed camps (notes p. 6)—series of crises (Morocco, Bosnia-Herz—notes pp. 3, 7, 9) Situation made worse by . . .

Para 4, and so on
Long-term causes (continued): Other sources of international rivalry—Quote (notes p. 4)—imperial rivalry (notes p. 6), naval rivalry (notes p. 7).

Final para
Conclusion: There were several causes.

When this plan is finished, you will know exactly which notes you are going to use to support what you are going to say, and in what order.

Keep a balance of information and ideas.
- Ideas are useless without the backing of evidence (facts). This may take the form of quotations, dates, names, statistics, and so on.
- Evidence is useless unless it is used to support an idea. There is no point in writing down the main events leading to the outbreak of war in 1914 unless they are used to support a **thesis**.

Do
- Stick to your plan.
- Use your own words, unless giving a quotation that you acknowledge.
- Try to make the first sentence of each paragraph, especially the very first paragraph, as arresting as possible.
- Present statistical information in the form of a table, graph, or other type of graphic organizer. See the example of a Venn diagram on page 50.

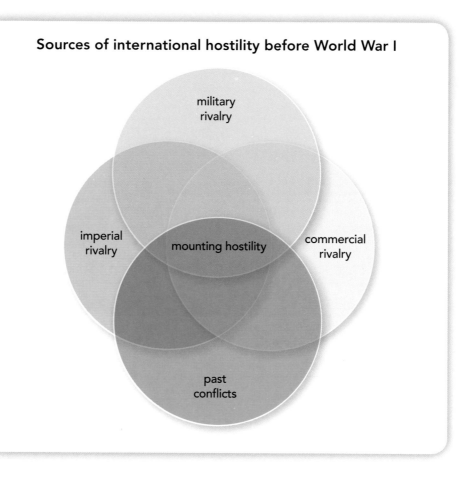

Sources of international hostility before World War I

- military rivalry
- imperial rivalry
- mounting hostility
- commercial rivalry
- past conflicts

- Give the source of each quotation, unusual opinion, or statistic. This can be done in one of three ways:
1. Within the text—for example, "Lenin said that the Great War was a capitalist conflict."
2. Using parentheses—for example, "The Battle of the Somme has become an epitome of the Great War (J. M. Bourne, *Britain and the Great War, 1914–1918*, New York: Edward Arnold, 1989, p. 65).
3. With **footnotes**. A footnote is a way of telling the reader the precise source of a piece of information—usually a quotation—as soon as it is given. It involves putting a small number immediately after the words the reader wants to source. The number is repeated at the bottom of the page or as part of a list at the end of the piece (endnotes), and next to it the source is given. Here is an example from Holger H. Herwig's *The First World War: Germany and Austria-Hungary 1914–1918*, New York: St. Martin's, p. 6:

In Salzburg, an Austro-Hungarian court martial found the draft dodger Adolf Hitler . . . unfit ("too weak; incapable of bearing arms") for military service.[2]

Herwig's footnote citation for this is:
[2]Werner Maser, *Adolf Hitler. Legende, Mythos, Wirklichkeit*. Munich: Bechtle, 1974, p. 12.

By this means, readers are told precisely where the author found his information—and, if they wish, they can check it for themselves. This is part of the system used to prevent fraudulent scholarship.

Avoid the following:
- The first person singular ("I"). This is too informal.
- Underlining for <u>effect and emphasis</u> —your words are your power.
- The passive tense where possible—for example, say, "Colonel Lawrence led the attack" rather than "the attack was led by Colonel Lawrence."
- Slang—for example, "Brusilov was the coolest general on the Russian front."
- Unnecessary foreign/jargon/long words—"The plan's raison d'être was . . . "
- Exaggeration for effect—for example, "Millions died in that battle."

Bibliography
At the end of your paper, include a bibliography or list of sources you have used.

Books are usually set out like this:
Author's last name, first name or initials. *Title of Book*. Place of publication: publisher, date of publication.
Example: Feldman, Ruth Tenzer. *Chronicle of America's Wars: World War I*. Minneapolis: Lerner, 2004.

Websites are set out like this:
Author's last name, author's first name or initials [if available]. "Title of Article." Title of Website. Web address (date accessed).
Example: Strachan, Huw. "World War I." World Book.com. http://www.worldbook.com/wb/article?id=ar610440&st=world+war+26 (accessed September 20, 2008).

There are specific styles for other sources, such as articles and encyclopedia entries. Ask your teacher if there is a particular style or way of organizing your references that you should use.

Your finished project
When you have finished your work, read it through very carefully. Better still, get someone else whose opinion you value to read it through.

Glossary

5 Ws test technique for examining a resource, asking: Who produced it? What exactly is the evidence it offers? When was it written? Where was it created? Why was it created?

allegiance loyalty to a region, country, person, or cause

Allies group that fought against the Central Powers (see below). The principal Allies were France, Russia, Great Britain, Italy, and their empires, joined in 1917 by the United States.

anonymous of unknown authorship

Anzacs Australian and New Zealand Army Corps

archive store of documents

armistice suspension of hostilities by those involved in a war

attrition warfare to wear down the enemy rather than defeat them in a single battle

Austro-Hungarian Empire large empire in central Europe, ruled by the Habsburg family

Balkans politically unstable area between the Black Sea and the Adriatic

bibliography list of reading materials—principally books—on a subject

Bolsheviks Russian communist group that seized power during the October 1917 revolution

bunker large underground shelter made of concrete and steel

censorship when an authority (such as an army officer or a government) checks all media output, letters, and so on, and removes or bans anything it considers damaging

Central Powers Germany, Austria-Hungary, and their allies (principally Turkey) in World War I

conscription military service that is compulsory (required by law)

database online tool containing information from a range of sources and links that are selected and developed for a specific audience. Most are subscription services that require membership or payment.

disillusioned disappointed, let down

document in history, a piece of writing providing evidence

entente understanding or agreement between nations that is less formal than a treaty. The *Entente Cordiale* was a friendly agreement made between the United Kingdom and France in 1904.

evaluate in history, the process of figuring out the importance of a piece of evidence

evidence in history, anything that helps create an accurate picture of the past

footnote material additional to a piece of writing. It is set out separately and linked to the main body of text by a number. When listed together at the end of a work, they are known as endnotes.

front region where two hostile forces are in conflict, such as the Eastern Front in World War I. World War I also saw the introduction of the term "home front," indicating how all the citizens of a warring state were drawn into the conflict.

imperial relating to empires. An empire is a group of countries under the control of one powerful country.

interpret in history, to figure out what to make of a source, usually written, whose meaning is not immediately obvious

KWL system for checking that one's research is on track: what I **K**now, what I **W**ant to know, what I have **L**earned

memoir written memories of an event or period of time

Mesopotamia modern-day Iraq

mutiny rebellion against those in charge

objectivity practice of judging, as far as is possible, purely on factual evidence and not on emotion

offensive large-scale attack

Ottoman Empire huge empire in the Middle East based around the area that is modern-day Turkey

plagiarism dishonestly passing off someone else's words and/or ideas as your own

propaganda material deliberately slanted to give a less-than-accurate picture of a situation. It may be positive, reflecting well on the writer's own side, or negative to reflect badly on the enemy.

reparations payments made as compensation for damage done

shell-shock word used during World War I to mean a mental breakdown brought on by the stress of serving in the front line

source anything that gives information about a period in the past. A primary source dates from the period itself, while a secondary source has been produced afterward.

Soviet committee of revolutionaries in Russia

SQ3R system for getting the most from a document: Survey it, ask Questions about it, Read it carefully, Recall (or Recite) its main points, Review what you have learned

survey in history, to read over quickly

thesis idea put forward for consideration

total war war involving all of a nation's resources, human and material

verbatim word for word

Find Out More

Further Reading

Many books have been written about World War I, so some of them are not very good! Here are some of the better ones.

For students

Allan, Tony. *20th-Century Perspectives: The Causes of World War I*. Chicago: Heinemann Library, 2003.

Bosco, Peter I., and Antoinette Bosco. *America at War: World War I*. New York: Facts on File, 2003.

Evans, David. *Teach Yourself: The First World War*. Chicago: McGraw-Hill, 2004.

Feldman, Ruth Tenzer. *Chronicle of America's Wars: World War I*. Minneapolis: Lerner, 2004.

Hamilton, John. *World War I: Trench Fighting of World War I*. Edina, Minn.: ABDO, 2004.

Ross, Stewart. *Timelines: World War I*. Mankato, Minn.: Smart Apple Media, 2007.

Taylor, David. *20th-Century Perspectives: Key Battles of World War I*. Chicago: Heinemann Library, 2001.

Adult books that students might find useful

Strachan, Hew, ed. *Oxford Illustrated History of the First World War*. New York: Oxford University Press, 2000.

Wiest, Andrew A. *The Illustrated History of World War I*. Edison, N.J.: Chartwell, 2001.

Literature

The authors of these classic works all experienced the war firsthand:

Brittain, Vera. *Testament of Youth*. London: Victor Gollancz, 1933.

Graves, Robert. *Goodbye to All That*. London: Jonathan Cape, 1929, and many further editions.

Hemingway, Ernest. *A Farewell to Arms*. New York: Scribner's, 1929, and many further editions.

Remarque, Erich Maria. *All Quiet on the Western Front*. Boston: Little Brown, 1929, and many further editions.

Sassoon, Siegfried. *Memoirs of an Infantry Officer*. London: Faber, 1930, and many further editions.

Movies

It is interesting to view war movies after you have researched the war, seeing which are the most historically accurate.

The African Queen, 1952
All the King's Men, 1949
All Quiet on the Western Front, 1930
Farewell to Arms, 1932
Gallipoli, 1981
The Grand Illusion, 1937
Lawrence of Arabia, 1962

Original film and audio

There is a wide and informative selection of original film, audio, and songs at www.firstworldwar.com, and there's a link to the famous *Somme* film at www.iwm.org.uk/server/show/nav.00o003004004.

Websites

Two general subscription sites (sites that have to be paid for access) are:
www.britannica.com
www.worldbookonline.com

PBS's guide to World War I includes timelines, maps, and more:
www.pbs.org/greatwar/

An independent website, edited by Michael Duffy, has a fine range of primary source material:
www.firstworldwar.com/about.htm

There are excellent documents on this Fordham University website:
www.fordham.edu/halsall/mod/modsbook38.html

Museums to visit

Australian War Memorial, Canberra, Australia
Great War Flying Museum, Brampton, Canada
Imperial War Museum, London, United Kingdom
National World War I Museum, Kansas City, Missouri, United States

Index

56